Marilyn Manson

SMELLS LIKE WHITE TRASH

PHOTOGRAPHIC CREDITS

FRONT COVER © FRANK FORCINO © LFI

© ALL ACTION
(Pages: 33, 46, 51, 58, 61, 75, 78)

© LONDON FEATURES INTERNATIONAL LTD
(Pages: 11, 13, 29, 39, 43, 65, 72, 94)

© ANGELA LUBRANO
(Pages: 9, 23, 36, 42, 96)

© PICTORIAL PRESS
(Pages: 5, 20, 24, 54, 59, 86)

© REX FEATURES
(Pages: 14, 17, 21, 30, 68, 80, 83)

© STAR FILE PHOTO
(Pages: 18, 45, 90, 93)

First published in Great Britain 1997
UFO Music Ltd 18 Hanway Street
London W1P 9DD

The author and publishers have made every effort to contact all copyright holders. Any who for any reason have not been contacted are invited to write to the publishers so that a full acknowledgment may be made in subsequent editions of this work.

ISBN 1-873884-70-2

Designed by Peter Pek at Morning Star Media for UFO Music Ltd

Marilyn Manson.

SMELLS LIKE WHITE TRASH

BY SUSAN WILSON

CHAPTER ONE

When the nineties dawned, rock culture spat back in the face of glamour. Stripped down to its bare minimum, American rock began to embrace the punk ethic, and the pouting, posing predecessors of the eighties were booted into orbit. Authenticity was the name of the game, decadence was declared dead, and grunge ruled the world in all its blue collar glory.

Bands like Mötley Crüe, Poison, Skid Row, Warrant and White Lion found themselves on the scrapheap, glittering like unwanted cracker trinkets after the novelty's worn off. Once the darlings of Hollywood, whose Sunset Strip echoed with the clacking of cowboy boots and the sleazy anthems of the glam rock years, these bands, with their teased up hair, their perfectly applied lipstick and their leopardskin lycra were suddenly completely redundant, thanks to a handful of scruffy kids from the northwest. Almost overnight, Hollywood lost its undeniably tacky charm. Rock fans no longer identified with silly sex, drug and rock'n'roll traditions which lent them nothing but beat-up escape routes from humdrum existences. They wanted something more real, something more tangible, something which related to their own experiences. The Reagan generation had given way to Generation X, a youth without a vision or even a goal, and they didn't want to look for broken dreams inside a can of hairspray on

smells like..

their way to Tinsel Town. They wanted to hear their emptiness echoed back at them. They wanted to feel understood.

Out of all of the bands dealing in the new language of reality, Nirvana were by far and away the biggest success story. Part of a tightly knit community of musicians all based around the Seattle area who got their kicks at keg parties in the woods and whose wardrobes consisted of shabby Levis and faded flannel shirts, Nirvana took grunge into the mainstream, sneering at it all the way along. Irony, sarcasm, intelligent digs at the very people whom he was addressing, coloured Kurt Cobain's songs and elevated them into a dimension all of their own. Kids recognised his perspective instantly, seeing in it their own frustrations with society, and while eventually, a huge faction of Nirvana fans were simply bandwagon jumpers without a care for the essence of what the band were actually saying, a vast number were listening very carefully. Other bands, like Mudhoney, Screaming Trees, Soundgarden, Tad and Alice In Chains all enjoyed major label success, but not to the level Nirvana reached. Kurt Cobain, Nirvana's supremely talented songwriter and frontman found himself, albeit reluctantly, in the position of icon, of generational spokesperson. His anti-rock star stance, his personal story of broken

...THEY DIDN'T WANT TO LOOK FOR BROKEN DREAMS INSIDE A CAN OF HAIRSPRAY ON THEIR WAY TO TINSEL TOWN. THEY WANTED TO HEAR THEIR EMPTINESS ECHOED BACK AT THEM. THEY WANTED TO FEEL UNDERSTOOD.

homes, waywardness and bitter, slacker punk sensibility, which paradoxically despised itself spoke volumes to millions of kids just like him, and he became a hero in a world full of lies.

It was good, if not glorious for a while – this pure white anger, these delicious songs, this great big fuck you in the face of despair – but it couldn't last. Nirvana may have altered the traditions of rock culture for the best part of a decade, and in some ways for good, but ultimately something had to give. Grunge couldn't sustain itself, and while Cobain's suicide was interpreted by many as some kind of huge symbolic statement of the genre's impotence and inability to fully confront and take on the world it so contemptuously rejected (when in fact his death was rather the result of depression, mental and physical pain, a personal sense of failure and lack of control and of course a heroin addiction), the real reason it didn't last was because the demands of time had changed yet again.

Of course without Cobain, grunge (for want of a better term – this one died a death the minute the media laid claim to it) couldn't continue in all of its previous glory. Bands left to carry on the legacy – like the multi-million selling Pearl Jam for instance – felt the full blow of Cobain's death on a personal level, and as musicians they continued to grow and evolve away from the simplistic, although highly effective punk/seventies rock blend – if indeed that's what they'd ever indulged in. At least without the umbrella of 'grunge' threatening to homogenise them, these bands could now concentrate on carving out individual identities. But the genre's main failing was its insistence on political correctness, its social conscience and its inability to ultimately see entertainment as entertainment period.

Bands like Nirvana, Soundgarden and Pearl Jam came along at a time when they were sorely needed. They addressed a different set of issues and altered the whole climate of rock culture, making it more amenable to women, opening up debates and

...REZNOR HAD DONE FAR MORE THAN SIMPLY SIGN UP ANOTHER STATESIDE NOVELTY ACT. FAR FROM IT. HE'D JUST LAID HIS HANDS ON THE VERY NEXT SUPERSTAR. THE ANTICHRIST SUPERSTAR, NO LESS.

reaching out to people who'd been left cold by thigh-high boots and poodle perms. They'd lent substance to rock, both musically and ideologically. But when the whole thing went up in a po-faced, heroin-addled big black puff of despondent smoke, with bands like Alice In Chains singing of drug-laden nightmares and then being forced to put their career on hold because of their singer's addiction, fun looked like a long-forgotten and much-needed prospect. It was time for rock culture to embrace entertainment again.

Parallel to the grunge explosion of the early nineties, another cool manifestation of rock was busy burrowing its way through the tracks. At the beginning of the decade, Trent Reznor, a slightly peculiar, self-absorbed character from the industrial wastelands of Cleveland, Ohio was forging a sonic explosion of electronics and guitars. Welding emotion to technology, he became recognised as the ringleader of industrial rock, along with Ministry, Revolting Cocks, Thrill Kill Kult and a handful of other bands, most of whom had stepped out of Al Jourgensen's Wax Trax empire in Chicago. Reznor had played guitar with Revolting Cocks, but signed to Island Records with his own project, Nine Inch Nails, an innovative outfit who dressed in leather and Doctor Martens, dreadlocks and piercings, and who embellished on a post-apocalyptic Mad Max type vision for their videos. They swept through Britain and America in 1990 with their debut album, *Pretty Hate Machine* and its hit single, 'Head Like A Hole', although thereafter the momentum died out, giving way to grunge, and taking a backseat until further down the line when swarms of American bands beefed up their sound with similar beats. Reznor put out two more releases, *Broken* and *The Downward Spiral*, and while 1997 has promised to deliver his next full length album, he's spent the last few years producing bands and starting up a record label.

In 1993, one band in particular caught Trent Reznor's eye. Trading in the sort of neo-goth Nine Inch Nails had adopted, this band went twenty or so stages further. Caked in make-up, decked out in leathers and scars, sporting names taken from serial killers and sex goddesses, Marilyn Manson, as the band were known, (named after their lead singer) captured Reznor's imagination with their showstopping personas and grinding industrial-metal beats. He was so impressed, he snapped them up and signed them to his label, Nothing, which was licensed by Interscope. Maybe he knew it, maybe he didn't, but Reznor had done far more than simply sign up another Stateside novelty act. Far from it. He'd just laid his hands on the very next superstar. The Antichrist Superstar, no less.

THE BEAUTIFUL PEOPLE

chapter two

marilyn manson

14

the beautiful people

*r*ock has never stood still as an artform. It constantly reinvents itself, pinching bits from its own past, rummaging through its own dressing-up box to conjure up new spins on old tricks, both sonically and visually. Entertainment is always the keyword, and whether or not this requires hefty elaboration depends upon the taste of the times and the effectiveness of the artist. Some rock stars simply strap on a guitar and belt out the tunes without bothering to change their T-shirts, perpetrating the tradition of Nirvana. But others deliver unbelievable visions, promising dreams and nightmares, faraway places, cartoons made flesh and fantasies incarnate. The stuff of make believe made real, some may find faintly ridiculous, but it never fails to attract attention.

There is a long legacy of rock stars who've indulged in the realms of fantasy. The Rolling Stones did it in the sixties, with their sumptuous costumes and acid laced *Beggars Banquet*. David Bowie did it, reinventing himself as Ziggy Stardust, an exotic, androgynous creature who looked as if he'd fallen from the sky. Marc Bolan did it during the glam era, Jimi Hendrix and Syd Barrett did it during the psychedelic era, and Alice Cooper and Kiss did it during seventies' America, when platform boots, silver make-up and fake blood fuelled all kinds of teen dreams.

In Britain, rock subcultures have always had particular influence. From the days of the Teds, Mods and Rockers, right through to hippies, punks, goths and rude boys, up to present day dance culture, tribes have given adolescents an identity to wear, a place of belonging. America, being a much bigger and more diverse culture, has never really harboured the same sort of mentality. Kids follow bands and dress up, but they don't divide themselves up quite so neatly into different social groups. There are subcultures in the States, but they don't have the same resonance, and usually, they take their cue from Britain, even if (as in the case of punk), their origins lie at home.

It's easy to spot the influences of British youth culture on American rock culture though. Punk was hugely significant in the whole grunge phenomenon, and in more recent years, the whole Goth thing has really taken ahold. Goths originated in Britain during the eighties. Inspired by bands like The Mission, Sisters Of Mercy and Southern Death Cult (later The Cult), Goths immersed themselves in nineteenth-century literature (Edgar Allan Poe, Bram Stoker, Mary Shelley), dressed in black lace and leather, pointed boots and buckles and big frilly shirts, dyed their hair black, spiked it up or knotted hair extensions into it, and applied ridiculous amounts of panstick make-up, thick black kohl and black lipstick. The scene tended to attract the socially dysfunctional, with its emphasis on the strange, and many previously shy, awkward people, found themselves a niche at last – together with narcissists and exhibitionists, curiously enough. Goths were the butt of jokes, especially when they sat on library steps in town centres, hung around college canteens or caught the last bus home – doubtless because their appearance, being so extreme, was deemed to be preposterous by those less in need of drawing

THE BEAUTIFUL PEOPLE

marilyn manson

18

attention to themselves in such a perverse manner. But they were tenacious and deadly serious about their lifestyles. Goth nightclubs flourished, and even when the genre died an official death, many who'd been involved found it difficult to let go of the look and the sensibility altogether.

When Nine Inch Nails resurrected the image of Goth in 1990, they were initially appealing to a homegrown audience who'd become fed up with the bubblegum rock-pop of Hollywood, but who weren't about to be satisfied by a bunch of ordinary looking longhairs from Seattle. Despite the enormous popularity of Nirvana and their contemporaries, there was still a place in rock culture for something beyond the norm. Something outside of the sphere of familiar, everyday experience. Nine Inch Nails captured the imagination of America, and fed it with something sinister, sexual and skewed. They employed artifice with style, entwining their fetishistic image in hollow lyrics of almost unbearable pain, yet at the same time, giving vent to anger with their snarling sonic rage. Fusing dance beats with out-of-control guitars, they gave Goth a new guise, dressing it up for the nineties, while hanging onto the miserabilism and the drama.

GOTHS WERE THE BUTT OF JOKES, ESPECIALLY WHEN THEY SAT ON LIBRARY STEPS IN TOWN CENTRES, HUNG AROUND COLLEGE CANTEENS OR CAUGHT THE LAST BUS HOME

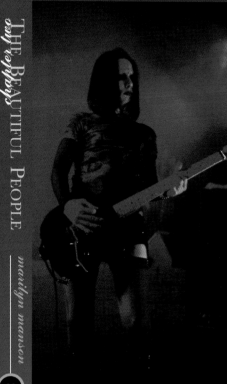

Americans liked Goth because it wasn't subtle. Nine Inch Nails gave them something to chew on, but the sheer spectacle of Marilyn Manson would fuel their thirst for sensation beyond compare. Manson's popularity lay in his unparalleled ability to stand out from the crowd, his knack for controversy and his love of the macabre. His entertainment factor was as big as it gets, and he quickly inspired a very large following of kids, all looking for a thrill and a route to rebellion. And it wasn't just his native country which was captivated. In Britain, a whole new generation was turned onto his shocking imagery, the larger than life spectacle, the entire fantastical nightmare. The original Goths were way too old to appreciate Manson, but it was easy to spot his influences, and while there were those who couldn't understand why anybody would want to revive such a ludicrous eighties idea, others, mostly those too young to remember the first time round, were riveted.

While Manson's British fans were undeniably as enthusiastic and as enthralled as his American ones, a great deal of his appeal was contextual with regard to the religious climate and moral codes which predominated throughout his homeland. America, being largely a Christian nation with extremely conservative beliefs and strict value systems (no matter how hypocritical), was the only possible breeding ground for a Marilyn Manson. The direct product of a twisted society, his entire persona was based on rebelling against an atmosphere of rigid polarities, dogmatic preachings, and overwhelming attempts to stamp out individualism. From a very young age, Marilyn Manson was determined to be different, to stand up and be counted, and he set out on a very focused path to prove his point.

CHAPTER THREE

*M*arilyn Manson began life as an ordinary young boy in Cleveland, Ohio. Christened Brian Warner, he was born in 1969, and spent the first 16 years of his life living in the industrial wasteland of America's east, growing up in the same, drab, depressing environment as Trent Reznor. Crowded with factories, all throwing out poison to the skies, Cleveland is hardly a place conducive to cheery childhoods, and Brian certainly didn't have one. He felt isolated and lonely, and although he wanted to be popular at school, he wasn't, so instead, he decided to withdraw into himself and nurture his own inner world.

One of the most formative aspects of Brian's younger years was his schooling. He was sent to a private Christian school where he was subjected to countless Bible study classes, and as a result of his indoctrination, he began to have nightmares about hell, fire and brimstone. He didn't fit in at all. In fact, he felt like a complete alien.

"At school, they drilled the ideas of Armageddon and the Anti-Christ into our heads for a few years and I had bad nightmares," Manson later told *Kerrang!*'s Steffan Chirazi. "I had the desire to ask questions but I was too afraid to actually do so.

wormboy

"I didn't have many friends because I was one of the few bad kids. I wouldn't bow my head for prayer. In fact, I'd steal money from the girls' purses when they were praying.

"I started misbehaving really badly because I wanted to go to a normal school. When I did get kicked out, all the kids in my new school wanted to kick my ass because they knew I'd been to private school."

He reiterated this story in an interview with *Q*'s Steve Malins.

"I was alone a lot as a kid. My parents weren't very strict but they sent me to a private Christian school. I was ostracised there and did my hardest to misbehave and get kicked out. There was one time when I put a vibrator in my teacher's desk..."

Speaking with *Melody Maker*'s Victoria Segal, Manson painted a slightly different portrait of himself as a school kid; "I wasn't a bad kid. I always wanted to be someone who was popular at school. But I wasn't. So I just kinda became invisible."

Whether he was good or bad, the young Brian certainly suffered from extreme feelings of otherness. And although he eventually managed to orchestrate his removal from his Christian school, the effect the institution and its indoctrination had on him was to last a lifetime.

"It all started when I was a kid," Manson said of his latter-day persona in conversation with *Kerrang!*'s Kevan Roberts, while on the road in Minneapolis with his band, reiterating what he'd told Chirazi. "I was so afraid of the apocalypse and the anti-

Christ mythology was something that completely terrified me. I worried constantly about what was going to happen to me.

"As I got older, as a payback to the people that terrified me when I was a kid, I decided that I was going to be the one to bring about an end to their world – though not necessarily my own."

Hence his eventual evolvement into the Antichrist Superstar as an adult rock star. Until that happened though, other influential factors on Manson's development, included finding a foetus in a can in the street when he was about ten, being nearly smothered with a pillow by an intruder who broke into the Warner family home when Brian was about eight or nine (since when he's never been able to sleep without a television on

"AS I GOT OLDER, AS A PAYBACK TO THE PEOPLE THAT TERRIFIED ME WHEN I WAS A KID, I DECIDED THAT I WAS GOING TO BE THE ONE TO BRING ABOUT AN END TO THEIR WORLD – THOUGH NOT NECESSARILY MY OWN."

somewhere in the background), his witness to his grandfather's bizarre sexual practices, and his prevailing ill health. As a child, he was admitted to hospital four times with pneumonia, experiences which added to his feelings of seclusion and resulted in his difficult personality.

"Being in hospital kinda warped me," he told *Select*'s Caitlin Moran. "You're around dying people; deformed people; disturbed people; artificial limbs on sore stumps. I collect artificial limbs now – it's one of my more recent hobbies."

"My childhood was no worse than anybody else's," Manson admitted to *Q*'s Steve Malins, before adding, "I was a sickly child. I was in hospital four or five times with pneumonia. Later, my mother became a nurse so I've always had a medical fascination. I've inherited my father's characteristics more. He's always been a salesman, furniture mostly, and I think there is a bit of that PT Barnum quality to what I do."

As a child, Manson used to ambush unsuspecting people by jumping out at them with Halloween masks hiding his face.

"Only to scare them and make them laugh. I wanted attention. My first actual performance on the stage was playing Jesus in a school play when I was six or seven. I wore a towel around my waist but I wasn't wearing any underwear because I didn't know any better. Some of the big kids whipped my towel off – one of those classic nightmares you have of being trapped naked in front of all your classmates. That was my first experience of being traumatised by Christianity."

As if Christianity wasn't enough, Manson was also traumatised by his own grandfather.

"He collected trains which he kept in the basement of the house," the singer recalled in his interview with Steffan Chirazi. "I discovered that when he had the train-set on, it was masking the sound of him masturbating to pornography. He had a really deviant porn collection – women with horses and ducks and pigs and every sort of thing you can imagine.

"It was exciting and scary at the same time. Me and my cousin used to spy on him, and it became our own sick joke. He had throat cancer, so he couldn't speak, he'd just bark. It was like something out of a horror film. There's a song on *Antichrist Superstar* called 'Kinderfelt' which explains how he helped to harden the shell around me when I come to look at families."

Speaking of his grandfather to Moran, Manson elaborated a little. "He'd wipe the spittle off with his handkerchief – the same one he masturbated into."

And to Malins he said, "My grandfather died a few years ago but my grandmother still lives there. I saw her four years ago and actually went down to the basement where my grandfather spent all his time masturbating and collecting deviant pornographic items. The train set was still there and there were all these rusty paint cans hanging from the ceiling. I opened them and they're still filled with 16mm porno movies. It's like a part of him is still there. Just thinking about it gives me a chill. He used to be a truck driver and there's a story about him being in an accident and when they took him to hospital he was wearing women's lingerie underneath his clothes."

In an interview with the *NME*'s Sylvia Patterson, he revealed further disturbing truths with a sexual bent.

"My grandfather used to masturbate to a lot of really dark pornography, bestiality, bondage, and he had a really large collection of women's clothing and wigs and all sorts of sex toys and I stumbled across this when I was about twelve. It made a real, big impact on me as a kid and changed, really formed, my opinions on sex.

"Also, I had some experiences with a neighbour who used to make me take my clothes off. It was an older boy. He made me play strange games with him but when I told my parents they confronted his family and they said I was lying, same thing with my grandfather. It was something no one really wanted to admit to. So I had a lot of suppressed anger because no one believed me."

Unsurprisingly, Manson was sexually an underconfident and slow developer. His parents never really took the time and trouble to sit him down and explain about the whole birds and bees process, although his father apparently promised to hire him a prostitute for his 16th birthday.

"I was really scared at that prospect because I was scared of prostitutes, so I tried my hardest to lose my virginity before I reached 16," he told *Kerrang!*'s Paul Brannigan in an illuminating interview all about his sexual experiences. "I managed it just before I turned 16 and when I told my father it was too late for a prostitute to take my virginity, I think he was a little disappointed. Knowing my father, I think he was serious about that idea. Losing my virginity wasn't particularly special though. It was kinda quick and ugly and the girl wasn't very pretty so it wasn't a momentous experience. I took her out to this deserted park one night and we lay down on the grass on the baseball ground and did it. I think that experience is part of the reason I don't like sport."

As a teenager Manson found little popularity with the opposite sex. He ended up feeling bitter, if not a little twisted.

"I went through a bit of a misogynist period because I was resentful that I didn't have any luck and I had a big heartbreak – but then I turned to writing and started the band, and that became my escape from worrying about girls. When you listen to our early songs, there are a lot of spiteful lyrics about relationships which come from that period.

"Discovering sex through pornography probably gave me a warped view of sexuality and I kind of dislike pornography now. I'm kind of embarrassed and not excited about topless bars and things like that."

As with many kids full of frustration at the unfairness of the world, sick of being misunderstood, tired of failing with girls, and needing some sort of connection to prevent them feeling absolutely and utterly cut off from more or less everyone and

everything, Brian Warner found music to be his sanctuary from everything, not just the opposite sex. His first musical memory, as reported to *Kerrang!*'s Ray Zell involved a babysitter and Creedence Clearwater Revival and probably didn't make much of an impression on him artistically, although he did recall the incident with alarming clarity.

"I was about five or six. I remember my parents going away to Mexico City, and I was left with a babysitter. I remember listening to Creedence Clearwater Revival's 'Suzy Q' and I remember not wanting to eat my food. So I hid it in the back of the television. It probably rotted there. Hence the term TV dinner. I invented it."

Manson's strict Christian school had also inadvertently affected his musical inclinations.

"They really discouraged us from listening to music," he said in an interview with *Guitar World*. "Once, they had a seminar where they said, 'Now this is the type of stuff you can't be listening to'. They held up albums by Black Sabbath, Queen, Led Zeppelin... and played them backwards. Immediately, of course, this is what I became interested in listening to, because I wanted to know why they didn't want me to hear it. One thing I didn't realise was that my parents had the first Black Sabbath album in their collection.

"When I first put that first Sabbath album on, it scared me a little bit. It was dark, in its sound and in what was being said. I was immediately attracted to it. I guess that was the part of me that really wanted to get it, because it felt like that had been suppressed for so many years. It kind of just opened me up. I've said this before; Black Sabbath was my introduction to heavy metal."

As Manson grew older, music really took ahold of him. He immersed himself in the power of extreme artists – musicians who'd invented alternative personas for themselves, rock stars who'd swollen beyond the usual limits of humanity. And he also lost himself in the fantasy flights of Dungeons and Dragons, a game involving small figurines, careful strategy and plenty of imagination.

"Musically, Black Sabbath, Kiss, David Bowie and things that were way out all became very important," he informed Steffan Chirazi. "Then when I was 12 or 13, playing Dungeons and Dragons was a big thing. It was also considered very bad for kids in America – people were blaming it for everything from children killing themselves to cult associations."

His immediate parents were also part of Manson's disaffectation. His mother was a

"THE NAME MARILYN MANSON WAS SOMETHING THAT I USED TO DESCRIBE WHAT I WAS WRITING BECAUSE OF THE DICHOTOMY BETWEEN BEAUTY AND UGLINESS. IT PERFECTLY DESCRIBED MY INTENTIONS."

nurse and his father was a Vietnam vet who was one of a team deployed to spray the horrific chemical known as Agent Orange during the Vietnamese war. Agent Orange destroyed Vietcong, burning the local people and ruining all the plant life. This, together with Manson's distrust of brainwashing religions, and his increasing awareness of the corruption of politics and the mass media through which it was fed, made him thoroughly suspicious of the world in which he lived.

"Growing up, I read about the conspiracy theories like JFK and the Vietnam war and how so many of the stories were repressed," Manson told Steffan Chirazi. "My father was in Vietnam as part of a secret organisation called 'Ranch Hand', and they were the ones who sprayed Agent Orange on the foliage.

"He used to have to go to these military bases every couple of years for tests to see if it'd had any kind of adverse effects on him. They never came to any conclusions..." Manson's father was eventually demobbed and found himself a new career as a furniture salesman, although he and his son continued to be called in for government medical tests to see whether or not their DNA had been affected by the chemical. Manson was diagnosed as having an obscure heart condition, something which had obviously contributed to his ill health as a child.

"I remember being around a lot of crippled and disfigured people when I was young," he told Steve Malins. "My father and I would go to these gatherings of families from the Vietnam War and there were a lot of people who were allegedly affected by Agent Orange. There were kids with birth defects and I had to hang around them as a child."

When you consider the haunted tangle of Brian Warner's formative years, it's hardly surprising that Marilyn Manson emerged from the wreckage. Without developing an alter ego, Brian could easily have wound up shy, socially inept, sexually maladjusted and ridden with hang-ups and unhealthy complexes. Some people manage to survive whatever life chooses to throw at them, but they all have different strategies, and whether they sink or swim very much depends on the route they choose. Brian knew Marilyn Manson would save him from an early age. It was simply a matter of when and quite how his inner warrior would emerge.

It was during his late teenage years that Marilyn Manson really came to save Brian.

"Marilyn Manson has consumed me since the day he was invented," the star told Steffan Chirazi. "I can't write something unless it's a song. I can't draw something unless it's intended for use with the music.

"I don't have a separate hobby or life, and I feel more comfortable onstage than anywhere else. I often feel like I'm putting on an act when I have to 'behave' in everyday society.

"The big key to it is that when you're role playing, you can be whoever you want to be. Which is what Marilyn Manson became to me. I didn't want to be me anymore. Not because I was ashamed of myself – I just had the desire to be something different."

"Marilyn Manson was something I created," he told Victoria Segal, "and at some point there was no definition between creator and created. It just became everything

that I was. I didn't change the way I was thinking, I just kinda gave a name to it.

"Marilyn Manson gave me the strength to believe what I was saying. The Nietzschean ideal of the will to power always appealed to me as a kid. I've always been very determined, never accepted failure. "

"I had lots of different ideas but no real way to express them," Manson explained to *Kerrang!*'s Kevan Roberts. "And I decided that music would be the way to make them last forever.

"The name Marilyn Manson was something that I used to describe what I was writing because of the dichotomy between beauty and ugliness. It perfectly described my intentions."

And talking to *Kerrang!*'s Ray Zell, Manson re-emphasised the symbolic value of his chosen name.

"There's usually a Marilyn or a Manson present. Different people who I'm friends with either call me one or the other. It seems like Marilyn is the more, er, glamourous, Hollywood superstar element of my personality. And the more talkative, angry, violent side of me is always considered the Manson part."

Adopting such a strong persona can be problematic. The subject may wonder who people are really interested in – the real them, or their projected self. In Manson's case though, his persona had become him, so he wasn't worried about what potential sexual partners might be looking for.

"I'd actually prefer someone to go out with me because I'm Marilyn Manson: that's not a bad thing, it's a compliment," he informed *Kerrang!*'s Paul Brannigan. "If someone likes me for who I am now rather than who I was before, it's easier for us to get along.

"It's hard for me to deal with someone now who I knew 10 years ago. People's attitudes change a lot over the years, particularly when you're in a detached reality like mine."

But having said that...

"There are a lot of different dimensions to anyone's personality, and I have a lot of different moods and attitudes for different circumstances. So I'm not going to behave like I do onstage in bed. There's a time and a place for every part of me."

Before Marilyn Manson found his true vocation as a rock star, he made do with being a rock journalist. When he was 18, he left Ohio and moved to Fort Lauderdale in

Florida with his parents. In Ohio he'd been beaten up for being the skinny geek. He hadn't even mustered up the confidence to become a fully fledged Goth, despite being a fan of Alien Sex Fiend, Killing Joke and Bauhaus.

"I wasn't goth – I think maybe I wanted to be, but I wasn't cool enough to fit it. I didn't have the confidence," he confessed to Sylvia Patterson. "I was invisible, totally insignificant."

The move to Florida at least offered some hope of a personal reinvention, and when he began writing for his college newspaper about music, he started to discover a whole new world for himself – one which existed outside, as well as inside, his mind. Although of course, now that Marilyn Manson had come to roost, interviewing other people was far from ideal.

"I felt like I would rather have people asking me the questions," he continued, somewhat immodestly, to Patterson. "They never had the right answers."

In 1990, he managed to interview Trent Reznor of Nine Inch Nails. The meeting was a fateful one, and the pair swapped telephone numbers. As a result, Manson's then band, Marilyn Manson And The Spooky Kids, ended up supporting Nine Inch Nails on a club tour, with Manson occasionally taking to the stage without a stitch of clothing, and eventually Reznor signed Manson to his Nothing label, acting as co-producer on all of their releases, from the debut *Portrait Of An American Family* to the *Smells Like Children* mini album, and finally the *Anti-Christ Superstar* 'industrial concept opus' of 1996. It may have taken several years, but in the end, Marilyn Manson became a star and found himself standing on top of the platform he'd always hankered after. Finally people were sitting up and listening to him. His thirst for power was beginning to be soothed.

CHAPTER FOUR

*e*ver since his inception into the public eye, Marilyn Manson has caused controversy of the finest order. This has not happened by accident. Manson courts trouble, he invites it, he thrives on it. It has helped him to sell records and concert tickets, it has enabled him to enter people's lives and disrupt their relationships with their parents (and as everyone knows, that's the truest mark of a rock star) and it has made him a rebel and a hero – an anti-hero – and he loves it.

Together with his band (bassist Twiggy Ramirez, keyboard player Madonna Wayne Gacy, guitarist Zim Zum and drummer Ginger Fish), Manson has upset entire cities full of parents and Christians across America. Outside one of his shows in Florida, a protester was spotted carrying a placard which read "Warning to all fornicators, pot-heads, masturbators, drunkards, feminists, pro-choicers, thieves, homosexuals, blasphemers, evolutionists, idolators, and especially hypocrites – JUDGMENT DAY IS COMING!!" The protester wasn't joking.

NBC, the American television channel, once publicised Manson as having a reputation for "satanic sex and drugs rituals". The band have had to hire defence lawyer Paul Cambria, who represented the porn merchant Larry Flynt (subject of the

man that you fear

movie *The People Vs Larry Flynt* which starred Woody Harrelson and Courtney Love) to fight freedom of speech cases for them, and Manson has had to hire a personal bodyguard who accompanies him everywhere for 24 hours of every day thanks to serious death threats issued by the more extreme of America's right-wing nutters. In the South of America, the situation is noticeably worse than it is anywhere else in the country. Shows have had to be cancelled in South Carolina to the cost of $40,000 ("Only Columbia in South Carolina managed to ban us. You see, I don't do anything illegal on stage," the singer told Q magazine), bomb threats have been issued and large police presences have often been needed at Marilyn Manson concerts. It hasn't been uncommon for performances to be videotaped by local authorities in search of obscene or profane material with which to charge Manson. Rumours in circulation have included sex, self mutilation, satanism and cruelty to puppies, thanks to the Internet and religious groups, although most of them have been utter fabrication. Manson has been arrested but never charged, and the only court action undertaken has been on the band's behalf in order to reschedule any shows which were subject to enforced cancellation. All of their applications have been successful.

At the beginning of 1997, Manson's American tour was plagued by bomb threats, gun frights and a prominent American politician condemning the band for their "immoral behaviour". The bomb threat took place at Caldwell in Idaho in January, and while no explosives were actually discovered at the venue, the general belief was that the scare was part of a carefully planned campaign by Christian fundamentalist groups to keep Manson fans away from the shows. They didn't succeed, the show went ahead as scheduled, and the triumphant Manson made his point by declaring to the crowd: "They tried to blow up the building. How fucking Christian of them!"

In Salt Lake City more trouble ensued when the band, due to play at the State Fair Park, were forced to change venues to Wolf Mountain because of worries about their image. When they eventually did play the show, a local nutcase attempted to smuggle a shotgun into the venue, although luckily he was found out before he managed to get through the doors.

To top it all, Oklahoma state's governor, Frank Keating, denounced the band and tried to persuade people to boycott their show at Oklahoma's State Fairgrounds because he believed Marilyn Manson to be "peddling garbage, they are clearly bent on degrading women, religion and decency, while promoting satanic worship, child abuse and drug use". He didn't succeed, but his attempts were symptomatic of an unthinking society unreasonably threatened by particular forms of entertainment. Marilyn Manson himself has certainly never had any time for such blatant hypocrisy, and has delighted in making his views clear whenever possible.

"I've found that best crowds we've had were in Salt Lake City, Oklahoma City... all these places where there was so much resistance against us playing," Manson told *Guitar World*. "The audiences were great. It was so worthwhile to go there. It was like missionary work. I've always compared what we do to Christianity, in its own way.

"I had an interesting thing happen in Texas – I think it was in Lubbock, Texas. I like to have oxygen off to the side of the stage when I'm performing, and the paramedics refused to give me oxygen because of who I was. The people had to force them to. Because they were Christians they didn't want to help me. I didn't think that was very Christian of them.

"Everyone in America feels so guilty, they have to put on this pseudo Puritanism. TV makes you feel that you don't fit in if you don't buy the right kind of shampoo. And these religions make you feel guilty – that if you don't believe in their God, you're not going to their heaven. And that's why everyone's so miserable. If people would just relax, and enjoy art and music more, they would be happier."

"In America, Christianity is something people put on like a hat," he emphasised to *Melody Maker*'s Victoria Segal. "If someone like me comes to town, and it's going to

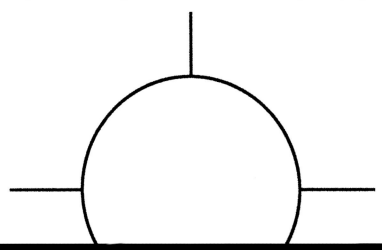

make them look good for an election year, give them a reason to have a fundraiser, or get some money, people rally behind an idea like Christianity. I'm not someone who worships the Devil or disagrees necessarily with what's written in the Bible – I just don't like the way Christianity victimises a lot of people. I'm not trying to say I'm Elton John and that what I do isn't offensive to some people, but I'm not doing anything illegal most of the time. This is America and you're allowed to have an opinion. I don't stand out in front of Sunday schools or set churches on fire – I'm just presenting my views which a lot of people are starting to agree with. People who are protesting don't see the irony in what I'm saying.

"With an idea like sanity or morality it's really just a case of what is popular. If you were to say, 'I was abducted by UFOs' most people would think you were crazy, but if you say 'I talked to Jesus through my toilet' they say it's a miracle."

When Sylvia Patterson went to Utica to interview Manson for the *NME*, another bomb threat was issued, while people were appearing on the television declaring Manson to be the Devil, no less. The bomb threat was something like the 60th on the 'Dead To The World' tour which had begun in the States in October 1996.

"I guess this is as far as you can go," Manson told Patterson of his Anti-Christ persona. "But I feel like somebody had to go this far. Anti-Christ is a kind of universal term, I don't even think it has so much to do with Christianity, I think it's just an opposition to the mainstream, an interesting idea. I may be this Anti-Christ that everyone thinks is so bad, but is that any different to what you are?

"It's all about perspective, it's about trying to show people that good and evil are really what you like and what you don't like and everybody has a different opinion so you can't have one universal definition of evil because everyone has their own taste.

"The first few things I like to establish with America and Christianity in particular, first of all, if you don't like what I am, complain to the manufacturer. It's your God that has created me. If they feel so strongly about their beliefs they shouldn't feel so threatened by one rock star. But it is a compliment to the acknowledgment of the power that I have. It's flattering when they cause such a fuss."

He also admitted that he was a member of the Church of Satan.

"I'm a member of the Church of Satan and I'm still a member of St Paul's

Catholic Church in Ohio, my main influence and something I never officially left. I've considered myself for the past six or seven years to be an occult scientist of sorts."

Speaking with Steffan Chirazi, Manson brought up his Nietzschean ideals again.

"My personal beliefs have always been based on Nietzsche's will to power – the idea of Satan and God being two words like Marilyn and Manson, describing different sides of your personality.

"I absolutely have a code of ethics which are sometimes very similar to Christian ones. Where I differ is that I greatly disbelieve in the idea of pity. The strong survive and the weak are really only there for the strong.

"We live in such a confusing culture in America. You've got so many people full of political correctness – bitching on like, 'Why can't everyone just be equal and just get along'. Yet America is based on intense capitalism which basically says if you can get more money and power by getting one over the next guy, then go ahead."

"I also dislike the idea of loving everybody. It cheapens the idea of love. The things I care about and love I'd do anything for and the rest of it is something I have no concern for. To do a random act of kindness is like living on the edge for me."

In February 1997, *Kerrang!* magazine reported on a "frenzied campaign" set up by American TV evangelist Pat Robertson to discredit Manson. Robertson was claiming that the singer and his band were leading the nation's young generation into devil worship, and he was using his *700 Club* cable television show to call for a full boycott on the band's activities. He even produced a fact sheet titled 'Repulsive Rock Infiltrating Young Minds' which contained a list of reasons explaining why he believed Marilyn Manson were responsible for poisoning the minds of American kids.

"You better watch for your children and grandchildren," declared Robertson. "To these kids it's a kick, it's a rebellion... 'Let's Play Satan Worship'. They are like sheep without a shepherd and they're being herded."

Kerrang! then went to point out that one of Marilyn Manson's top-selling T-shirts bore the slogan, "The Lord Is My Shepherd"!

"The idea behind *Antichrist Superstar* is probably as old as the band itself," Manson explained to *Kerrang!*'s Kevan Roberts in Minneapolis. "The Antichrist isn't so much a person as it is everyone's increasing, collective disbelief in God.

"And it's just a matter of each time someone plays the record, hopefully it will trigger them to take one step further from Christianity and one step further to believing in

Man That You Fear

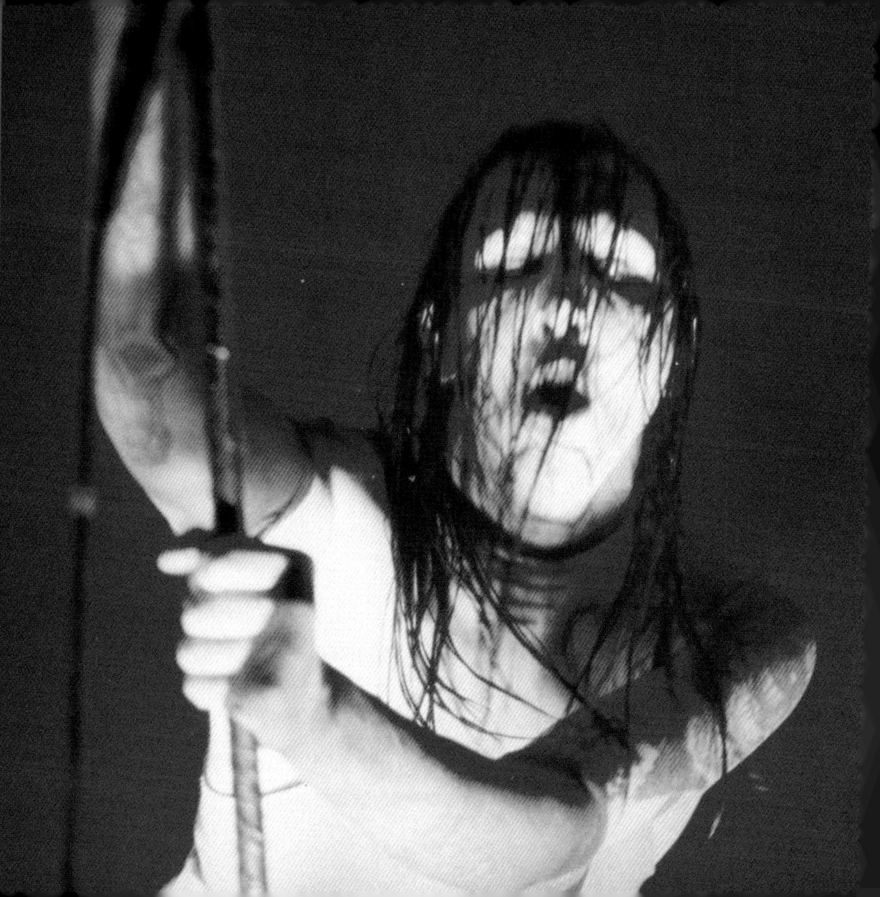

themselves and having a strong will.

"And for Christians, that is the Armageddon... but you know, for the rest of the world it might just be a fresh beginning.

"I see my revenge on the world happening. I even see it in the way these people probably hate the way their kids dress or the fact that they buy my records. But I never specifically sit down and and try and think up new ways to piss them off. Anyway, I'm sure my just being alive pisses them off enough as it is."

Talking to *Kerrang!*'s Ray Zell in Germany's East Berlin, Manson delved into his belief system again, pointing out the logic of his thoughts, and making it clear that he was more of an independent and selective thinker than an ignorant and potentially harmful devil worshipper. Yes he believed in faith, and yes he believed in hate and the power entailed in both, but he employed reason as well, even if the reasoning didn't always sound too friendly.

"If you really feel hatred for someone and kind of send it their way, then it is out of your system and in their hands. I always think it's therapeutic.

"The key is belief. Belief is very powerful, and it kind of dictates our reality. Say, for example, in America you've got a million people who have a Bible and are forced into accepting that reality is the fact that you have to worship God. But on the other hand, if I go and sell four million records and you believe what I've got to say then that becomes real. So, the idea of what's popular and what's real is interesting when you think about it.

"There's a lot of great stories and a lot of great values in the Bible, and I actually relate to a lot of them. The character, or the idea, or the part of my personality that I describe as Antichrist Superstar, is a lot like Lucifer in the Bible. Someone who was kicked out of heaven because he wanted to be God. I try to say in my story, 'Well, if it was told from his point of view, then would he still be the bad guy?'"

"The Bible is interesting and has a lot of important values and things like that in it," he told *Kerrang!*'s Kevan Roberts. "But the way people use it is where the problems lie.

"As for my own morality, the most outrageous thing I could imagine ever doing is putting on a pair of jeans and going to the shopping mall for my lunch. That would be pretty gross.

"At the moment I'm wearing this real rabbit fur. Someone gave it to me. That's another thing I hate, political correctness – it's just Christian morality disguised. The other day,

"I SEE MY REVENGE ON THE WORLD HAPPENING. I EVEN SEE IT IN THE WAY THESE PEOPLE PROBABLY HATE THE WAY THEIR KIDS DRESS OR THE FACT THAT THEY BUY MY RECORDS."

this girl gave me a hard time about wearing this coat, called me an asshole or something for 30 minutes, then asked for tickets to the show. That, I felt, illustrates how committed these people are to their little causes."

Despite Manson's philosophising, in America the trouble continued to worsen. The Bible Belt was determined to curb his career at any cost, and when lawsuits started to kick off again, the media went into overdrive.

Lawsuits involving rock music and the deaths of young kids have long been a feature of American culture. Judas Priest, the British metal band, were taken to court in a high profile case a number of years ago, and more recently, two hard rock record companies reached an out of court settlement after a woman called Donna Ream was shot by four teenagers in a convenience store in Oregon. The kids had been fans of Deicide and Cannibal Corpse, two bands from the death metal genre, renowned for their grisly lyrics, their links with evil and satanism and their highly aggressive, morbid music. Supposedly, the kids had been influenced by these bands into committing their crime, and while the record labels, Metal Blade and Roadrunner, refused to admit responsibility, they still awarded Ream with eleven million dollars. The implications for bands such as Marilyn Manson were beginning to look potentially bad, especially when a Californian family accused Manson of inspiring their 13-year-old son to commit suicide. Manson however, remained unmoved.

"The music's been designed to speak to the people who understand it and scare the people that don't," he explained to Andrew Smith of *The Sunday Times*. "People miss the irony a lot of the time. The type of behaviour that protesters are displaying, and

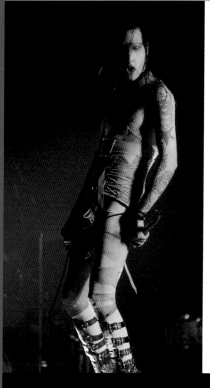

the kind of hostility and hypocrisy that they're showing, is the source of a lot of my lyrics. They always miss that. It's rewarding sometimes, because they ultimately prove my point with their ignorant responses."

Responding to the Donna Ream case with Metal Blade and Roadrunner, he expressed disappointment with what he perceived to be just another manifestation of American victim culture.

"I know I don't encourage the type of behaviour they're talking about. Usually what's happening is parents are looking for an easy explanation for a set of problems they don't understand and in which they probably play a large part. They're looking for someone to deflect the responsibility from themselves."

In an interview with Murray Englehart, reporting from Australia for *Kerrang!*, Manson spoke out about the rumours which had been levied against him in America. Already Australia had echoed the hysteria, although with a somewhat more positive tone than the States. No doubt this had something to do with the culture being altogether less uptight. *The Sydney Morning Herald* reported, 'An American rock band that has been accused of promoting paedophilia and whose members are named after infamous serial killers is coming to Sydney. It promises to be one of the most controversial tours of recent years...' *The Herald Sun* said, 'Marilyn has been arrested for stripping and burning Bibles onstage. The US needs this: with half the population in jails and the other half committing crimes, a wake-up call is required...' *The Daily Telegraph* said, 'Marilyn Manson's music is a mish-mash of seething industrial pop, bubbling with copious amounts of bile, sleaze and pure hate...' And *The Australian* said, 'The world's number one anarchist rock ghoul. If music be the food of upsetting your

parents, then the ear-crunching, relentless thrash and nihilistic lyrics of Marilyn Manson are just what the rock'n'roll doctor ordered...'

Despite the Australians' good humoured attitude, controversy still haunted Manson when one 15-year-old slashed her wrists with a penknife outside Melbourne's Palace theatre because she was too young to see her idol. She recovered after being rushed to hospital, but the incident can't have exactly helped Manson's heavily exaggerated reputation. While the man himself obviously understood the power and advantage of causing a stir, some of the whispers which dogged him were beyond the pale.

"The rumours tend to get further and further from the truth," he insisted in his interview with Engleheart. "They'll come on television and say that Marilyn Manson promotes anything from torturing animals to child abuse to raping your sister. It sounds to me like they pretty much say whatever they think will push people's buttons to rile them against us. It's kind of interesting.

"I don't really bother to defend myself, because people can say what they want, but our fans don't have a problem understanding what we're about. It's usually just their parents. It's the same as my parents were with Kiss, Alice Cooper and Black Sabbath, and as their parents were with Elvis. It's almost a tradition. The only thing I'd say to our fans is – remember this time when you're raising your own kids and try to understand your culture."

Manson went on to explain how his parents were in full support of what he did for a living now, despite their having sent him for religious education as a child. Apparently

they even had a shrine built to homage their son in their Florida home, with pictures of him all over the walls.

"Now my parents are big fans. I think it's because they understand it, because they saw me growing up. But I've never done anything to rebel against my parents. I've always been more dissatisfied with culture and society in general."

To *Melody Maker* he continued in a similar vein.

"My parents have become more and more like me because they're really fans of what I do. It's made them happier. They seemed to be much more miserable when I was growing up. It's so commonplace for parents to be divorced that it makes my family dysfunctional because mine are still together. My grandmother is very Catholic, very religious. I visited her just two weeks ago and she was very pleasant to me, she didn't chastise me. And I said, 'I'm going to Italy soon, so maybe I'll say hi to the Pope for you' and she said, 'Why don't you get him to kiss your ring?'"

When Caitlin Moran interviewed Manson for *Select*, she systematically asked him about some of the more vicious rumours which had been in circulation about him. Her questioning at times took on a certain level of ridicule, but in the light of the rumours themselves, it really wasn't so ludicrous. The British tabloid press had printed the more outlandish of America's beliefs about the star, so presumably Moran simply wanted to clear up a few things.

In November 1996, the *Sunday Express* reported, "The group's crowd-pleasing repertoire includes torturing animals onstage, smoking dried human remains, and performing depraved human sex acts... The band's members are devotees of the San Francisco-based Church of Satan, which believes in the ultimate triumph of evil."

The Daily Star reported, "Marilyn Manson – nasty, pro-violence, pro-perverts, sex crazed.... A debauched, Devi worshipping rock act from Florida – tagged the sickest band in America – plan to sneak into Britain."

And the *Manchester Evening News* reported, "Devil rockers Marilyn Manson's shocking performances have included outbreaks of violence, blasphemy and indecency..."

"In the British tabloids it was said that I vomit on the audience. That I torture pets onstage. That I smoke human shit." Manson smiled in conversation with *Kerrang!*'s Ray Zell. "I thought all three of those were really exciting because I've never done any of them. But I'm willing to try...."

On a slightly more serious note, when challenged by Moran, Manson denied ever having eaten human excrement, he denied ever having tortured baby animals and he explained the Sea Monkey drug story, which involved Smashing Pumpkins' frontman, Billy Corgan, and the smoking human bones story.

"Sea Monkeys are like little fleas that live in the sea. You can take them out of water and dry them into a white powder. You can leave them for years – but when they come in contact with moisture, they come alive again. Billy thought it was coke and he snorted it. He's gonna have little fleas living in his sinuses for two years. He's pissing out little prawns!

"We really did smoke human bones though. What happened was, when we lived in New Orleans, Twiggy and I had collected a big bag of human bones. They can't bury the dead properly in New Orleans – the ground is swampy and it shifts around. So, if you go walking in a graveyard, you'll see hands and leg-bones poking out. So we were carrying this bundle around for a while, like an extra relative or something. Then we were in LA with some people who thought they were hip. I don't particularly like people who think they're cool. So I convinced them that smoking bones was the new crack. Everyone chipped some off the bones and put them in the pipe. But it gave me an awful headache and it smelt like burn awful. Like burnt hair. Urgh."

Did Manson worship Hitler, Moran inquired. The reply was suitably irreverent.

"No. Ask me about 'The Wonder Years'. I was supposed to be in that as a child actor. That was another thing the tabloids have got all wrong. I'm supposed to have had two ribs removed as well, so I can give myself blow jobs! This stuff amuses me."

And what about simply being plain evil?

"I'm no more nasty or cruel than anybody. There's obviously two sides to everyone. I have a morality that's not that different from Christianity. Instead of turn the other

cheek, I believe in karma. If someone harms me, I want to harm them back – unless their life is so miserable that just waking up themselves is the greatest punishment. I don't feel a need to hurt people. I have an outlet for that – music. But there's subtle stuff that everyone misses, like the more… charming elements in someone like me. That people may like me and be affected by what I say."

Moran neglected to ask him about the depraved human sex acts. But Sylvia Patterson of the *NME* didn't. Allegedly, Manson had given one of Nine Inch Nails a blow job onstage.

"Their guitarist [Robin Finck] came onstage and pulled down his pants and was trying to embarrass us and I grabbed him and put his dick in my mouth and sent him on his way. So it wasn't really a full scale blow job, I don't even think his dick was hard so I don't know whether that counts. But my parents were in the audience and they didn't mind, so I don't know why anyone else should. Sex is so basic. It's all rock'n'roll to me."

Rock'n'roll does indeed provide plenty of opportunities for all kinds of peculiar sexual practices, and any rock musician will be bound to attract sexual attention to some degree. And a peculiar individual like Manson will have had his fair share of bizarre requests. Nine Inch Nails' Trent Reznor once confessed that he enjoyed watching groupies having enemas backstage, although Manson refused to admit to any such pleasures when speaking with *Kerrang!*'s Paul Brannigan.

"Those type of backstage shenanigans are interesting sometimes but they don't follow our band too much. And performing tends to be so draining for me, I don't have the

ROCK'N'ROLL DOES INDEED PROVIDE
PLENTY OF OPPORTUNITIES FOR
ALL KINDS OF PECULIAR SEXUAL
PRACTICES, AND ANY ROCK MUSICIAN
WILL BE BOUND TO ATTRACT SEXUAL
ATTENTION TO SOME DEGREE. AND A
PECULIAR INDIVIDUAL LIKE MANSON
WILL HAVE HAD HIS FAIR SHARE OF
BIZARRE REQUESTS.

energy to participate in much more than passing out after a show. I'm not the type of person to instigate things like that, but I'm voyeuristic so I'd be interested in watching. But I don't like to exploit people in that way; I'd rather exploit them through art on a grander scale."

And what of the child abuse allegations? It was back to Sylvia Patterson to clear them up.

"Any mention of child abuse has been me singing about my experiences with the

neighbour who used to make me take my clothes off. I use music as an outlet. So it's rather insulting when people think that I promote something like that. That's the type of childhood I had, not the type I would promote."

But didn't Twiggy Ramirez bring his 11-year-old brother onstage naked once?

"That's not really the case. His brother ran onstage once and mooned at the audience."

Animal abuse?

"Was that *The Sun*? You know I get mad when people say we kill dogs. I do have a dog, why would I want to kill a dog? I like dogs, I like nature, a snake doesn't apologise for itself, a squirrel is not looking for salvation."

Confirming his viewpoints on both child and animal abuse, Manson told *Kerrang!*'s Paul Brannigan, "I wouldn't support having sex with a child and I can't imagine having sex with an animal. When I was a kid I used to want to be a cat, because I was in love with my cat in a strange way. But I never had sex with it.

"Other than those things, I think most things are acceptable. There are things that I don't want to do sexually, but I don't actually morally disagree with them."

As for being pro-violence, it seemed that Manson's detractors were more violent than him.

"I think that the repression and guilt that revolves around sexuality causes sexual violence," he told Paul Brannigan. "We're so used to the Christian guilt that sex is dirty and masturbation will make you go blind, so people are ashamed to be themselves – which is more of a cause of sexual violence than pornography."

While he was being issued with death threats, bomb scares and having to employ bodyguards to search out gun-carrying maniacs, the only violence he was guilty of was onstage, between band members, and clearly part of the Marilyn Manson spectacle. Although as it turned out, things were getting pretty out of hand. Manson's original drummer, Sara Lee Lucas, left the band after the singer set both him and his drum kit on fire. His replacement, Ginger Fish, had to go to hospital after being belted by Marilyn's mike stand. And keyboard player Madonna Wayne Gacy almost bled to death after being hit by a flying microphone.

"It hit an artery and almost killed him," Manson calmly announced to *Kerrang!*'s Kevan Roberts, before adding, "It does get violent up there. Mostly I hurt myself in the heat of the moment. I can't feel it."

Onstage, Manson has smashed lightbulbs against himself and has repeatedly slashed his chest with broken bottles of wine, much to his mother's horror, and once he was jumped on by security staff for his antics and had to be saved by Glenn Danzig who was brandishing a baseball bat in order to fend off the bouncers.

Nevertheless, taken within the context of rock entertainment, albeit intense entertainment, even this violence was contained onstage, and part and parcel of the persona of the band. Manson has described his self mutilation as "more of a release" than some sort of weird, masochistic ritual, and also he's said that it "symbolises some of the pain that I sing about". Although once, in Hawaii, he passed out after "some glass went into an artery".

Even the band's names project a violent image, but in such an overblown manner that only a culture devoid of a sense of irony could have taken them seriously. Madonna Wayne Gacy was named after New York's biggest female star and John Wayne Gacy, a child murderer; Twiggy Ramirez was named after the top

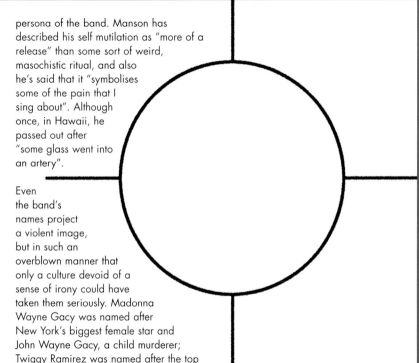

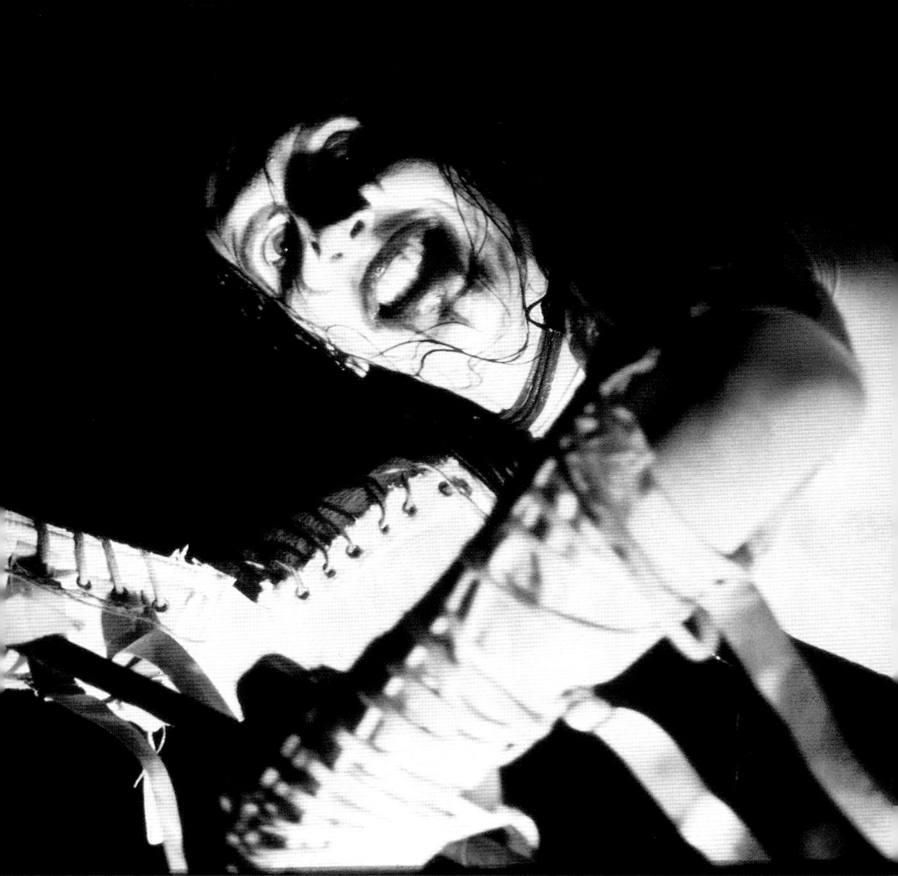

MAN THAT YOU FEAR

chapter four

sixties' model and the Night Stalker, Richard Ramirez; Zim-Zum received his title from an angel who did God's dirty work before the split between heaven and hell; and Ginger Fish took his name from Ginger Rogers and Albert Fish, a cannibal child killer. Obviously Marilyn Manson was named after Marilyn Monroe and Charles Manson.

With such a bizarre and imaginative image, not to mention all the controversy, the hype and the actual music, Marilyn Manson were bound to attract their fair share of nutters amidst their following. Even some of the death threats were coming from this lunatic faction of fans.

"The threats don't just come from the people you'd expect," Manson confided in *Kerrang!*'s Kevan Roberts. "Just the other night, a girl in the crowd tried to put a cigarette out in my eye. She just ran out of nowhere and started screaming at me. And she was a fan!"

"I've kind of looked into my idea of my own death on the record [*Antichrist Superstar*] so much that it made me numb to it and I'm not concerned with it anymore," Manson told Ray Zell. "I've more a fear of failure. To see the idea of Marilyn Manson die would be worse than to actually be dead.

"As for the death threats, I don't think about it too much because I've got to think of all the people who are there to enjoy it rather than the one person who is there to ruin it."

"Obviously I've asserted myself as an antichrist in my time," Manson told *Guitar World*. "So I'm sure there's a lot of people who, because of their belief in God, would feel it a duty or pleasure to put me in the ground. Those people make bomb threats at every show that we play, pretty much. But if I were to live in fear, I wouldn't be able to enjoy what I do. In fact, I think the sense of danger makes life more exciting for me."

The *NME*'s Sylvia Patterson found it hard to believe that anyone could really be so calm about having to live their life under such constant threat. But Manson merely reiterated, "It's the extreme balance of your life being threatened by so many and sought after by so many others. It's kind of exhilarating. Any life without the threat of death is not worth living. So many people are so concerned with what happens to them when they die, they never even bother to live."

And to *Melody Maker*'s Victoria Segal, who appeared to be impressed by the fact that Manson was attracting so much attention that people had actually threatened to kill him, he said, "It is satisfying but it becomes overwhelming when everywhere you go there's people making death threats and watching every move, waiting to arrest you."

But, Ray Zell wanted to know, what about the kids who were committing or threatening to commit suicide?

"I'd feel like they'd proven my point by misperceiving me. If somebody were to kill themselves or somebody else, that would just go to show how ignorant people are raised. You know, if they have to use a rock song as an excuse not to go on living, it's pretty weak.

"I'm creating music and I'm saying what's on my mind. How somebody relates to it is purely up to them. If people want to be like me, then they should be themselves because ultimately that's what I'm doing."

"I don't think people would have to be responsible for the things they create," Manson stated to Sylvia Patterson. "If some kid is carving himself up or trying to kill himself it's not because of music, it's because he's not understood by his parents. You're always going to initially emulate your idols, but I think that's the first stage of becoming yourself.

"I am about following your dreams but at the same time, when all of your wishes are granted, many of your dreams will be destroyed. Because Marilyn Manson is and thrives on extreme positive and negative together. I know that there's so many people who want to hear it and understand it and they're not even sure if they're supposed to hate it or not. I think that's an important part of culture, to keep people's minds going, keep the drains from clogging up.

"I don't think it's ambiguous. I think it's enigmatic."

CHAPTER FIVE

mister superstar

t he true culmination of Marilyn Manson's vision arrived with his *Antichrist Superstar* album in 1996. A hugely ambitious affair, it was divided into three stages, or cycles. Cycle one was called 'The Hierophant' after the Tarot trump, cycle two was 'The Inauguration Of The Worm', and cycle three 'Disintegrator Rising'. And yes, there was a heavy autobiographical bent which incorporated Manson's past, present and future. Sculpted from the dreams he'd had about his own life, general observations he'd made throughout his life, and the visions he'd had of his own death, the entire concept of *Antichrist Superstar* was pretty intense. 'Wormboy', in the second cycle metamorphoses into an the 'Angel With Scabbed Wings' until the wings fall off and the *Antichrist Superstar* of the final cycle emerges.

To achieve the right frame of mind with which to externalise his vision, Manson consciously starved himself of both food and sleep, and pumped himself with drugs, until he was mentally adjusted.

"The first time I stayed up for four days straight on crystal-meth, we started to put down the music to *Antichrist Superstar*," he told Chirazi. "And everything seems really different when you've been for four days on crystal-meth.

"In the end, I learned that I really didn't need to do drugs. I mean, eating spicy foods before you sleep really does enhance your dreams."

"When I made the record, one thing I considered was whether I'm giving myself the open-mindedness and the ability to predict what's going to happen in my future, or if we're creating it as we go along with my mere willpower," he informed Ray Zell. "Things like people saying the new album would debut at number one in the Billboard chart in the US, and I said, 'No, it's gonna be number three.' Because number three is a very powerful number on the album; it's repeated quite often. Then it did chart at number three. Was it a coincidence? You decide... If you're in touch with your subconscious you can really use it to your advantage.

"We recorded 'Irresponsible Hate

Anthem' on February 14, 1996. When that date comes around in 1997, it's gonna set forth a chain of events that will complete the ending of the album.

"A lot of people are expecting that day in both horror and anticipation. So..."

"We're about the basic principle of will-to-power," he told Sylvia Patterson, echoing what he's said in other interviews. "*Anti-Christ Superstar* is about being the biggest rock band in America and that's what I think Marilyn Manson is destined to be. The very fact that I've said it is is why it's going to happen."

Talking to Steffan Chirazi for *Kerrang!*, Manson compared *Antichrist Superstar* with his previous full length album, *Portrait Of An American Family*.

"I think I fell short originally, and this time the vision's much clearer and much more pure. For some people it will be easier for them to see *Antichrist...* as a concept record about this character, which is fine. But to me, it's much more real. It's my autobiography – about what's happened and what is going to happen to me."

"I've never talked about the things we've done," he said, somewhat more mysteriously in his *NME* interview. "Cos I feel it's kind of personal. I don't want to cheapen it. It was nothing like S&M, you just have to imagine the most terrible things you could do to yourself to release the chemical high in your mind. A lot of it was wrapped up in drugs..."

"My take on music has been the most subversive thing you can do, " he told Murray Engleheart. "Because by writing a pop song you become part of the mainstream and then there's a chance you might be able to get the mainstream to agree with something they don't necessarily want to because you've got them humming along to your tune. That causes people to be nervous."

In a society so driven by image, MTV has acquired a huge significance in the selling of rock music. Video has therefore become a major part of a band's repertoire. Marilyn Manson, being so visually oriented anyway, were bound to come up with some astonishing goods before long, despite the rather tacky packaging of their first few attempts. By the time it came to producing videos for "Sweet Dreams", the band's powerful cover of The Eurythmics' song, "Beautiful People" and "Tourniquet", the imagery had become truly sophisticated and highly impressive.

"I've always looked at everything I do as if this were my favourite band," Manson explained to Ray Zell. "I like to present things with every element possible – from the image to the music, to politics, to philosophy, to the religious aspects.

"We actually didn't spend as much money as you might imagine on the videos. The

thing that we've always done is, if you're given less money and less time to work, you're always more creative. And I've always liked to be a big part of the visual element of the videos – because it is us we're presenting, not just some director's idea of what the song is.

"'Beautiful People' is about challenging the

fascism of beauty. And I have a fetish for medical devices and I like to collect prosthetic limbs, so that's where all the props came from. I said to the director, 'I really want to incorporate that part of my personality into this video'. So together we dreamed up some imaginary items. Those devices are neither from the future or the past – they're from an unexplainable time.

"I hope that with our music we can inspire people to be creative and to use their imagination. Because it's something which is so lacking nowadays. You have virtual reality, MTV, video games and VCRs. Nobody wants to really think about things or create things. You have programmes on a computer which will write a poem for you.

"People say to me, 'You don't need to look like this or do this to your body, because we can do that to the picture on a computer. But it's not about that. It's about creating art."

Manson's belief in the power of art and the value of artists has fuelled his vision. He mentioned it in an interview for MTV's *Super Rock*, and has made it blatantly clear simply by doing what he does so effectively. There are those who have tried to dismiss

FOR SOME PEOPLE IT WILL BE EASIER FOR THEM TO SEE *ANTICHRIST*... AS A CONCEPT RECORD ABOUT THIS CHARACTER, WHICH IS FINE. BUT TO ME, IT'S MUCH MORE REAL. IT'S MY AUTOBIOGRAPHY...

Manson as some sort of trumped up pantomime act, no doubt on the basis of his early videos, his stark make-up and his revival of Goth imagery, but it's pretty hard to dispute the sophistication of his more recent videos, and no one could argue with the dramatic effect his stage show has on his fans. Not that Manson particularly cares what people think, because as with everything else, he has his own opinions on the whole "cartoon comedy-rock caper" thing.

"I think that's what Marilyn Manson has always been about," he told Sylvia Patterson, when she asked him if he cared about being regarded as a joke. "Pointing out that showbusiness is just such a fake thing and everyone is so full of shit. Marilyn Manson is a name that is so fake it goes beyond that and it becomes real. In a world that is completely full of lies it becomes the one lie that is worth believing."

If Manson didn't care what people thought of him, perhaps he was a very shrewd businessman, someone who'd spied a gap in the market, and liked the idea of not only making a fortune, but also of taking advantage of the fringe benefits afforded by the rock'n'roll lifestyle. Patterson put the question to the man.

"Even if I was just that," he replied, "that in itself is something to respect. People say to me, 'is what you do an act or is it for real?' and I think it's irrelevant either way. I think they should respect it for for whatever it is. People always look down upon performers with this notion of, 'is this what they really are?' And even if it's not what they really are, in the end it is what they really are because nobody else is doing it but them."

Certainly, nobody else has done what Manson's been up to. Although there have been bands who inject their stage shows with some elaborate theatrics, the Marilyn Manson live experience was a whole new ballgame. Appearing onstage in surgical corsets and stockings, his body covered in scars or streaming with blood from fresh wounds, his arms outstreched in a crucifix pose, his band swathed in dry ice, Manson cut a sinisterly memorable figure.

Perhaps the most controversial aspect of the entire set up was the 'Nuremberg Rally' section, where Manson appeared on top of a podium, wearing a black suit and a red tie, holding a Bible which he tore up and flung out to the audience. Behind him were two banners sporting the Marilyn Manson logo inside two parodies of swastikas. "We will no longer be oppressed by the power of Christianity!" he yelled from his elevated position.

"MARILYN MANSON IS A NAME THAT IS SO FAKE IT GOES BEYOND THAT AND IT BECOMES REAL. IN A WORLD THAT IS COMPLETELY FULL OF LIES IT BECOMES THE ONE LIE THAT IS WORTH BELIEVING."

Letting himself in for a whole heap of criticism, Manson again had answers to any questions concerning the dubiousness of such a stage set. Although the band didn't bring the podium to Europe in case they were "misinterpreted", Marilyn Manson appeared to know exactly what he was doing.

"A lot of the less intelligent journalists I've met have had trouble understanding certain elements of the show," Manson explained to Victoria Segal. "I'm trying to satirise the fascism of Christianity, of politics, of rock'n'roll, to point out that just as people follow Billy Graham or Bill Clinton, so is the danger they follow Antichrist Superstar. People mistake me for a pro-Nazi, for being hateful. I like to keep people thinking, not to

stop them from thinking."

In his interview with *Guitar World*, Manson spoke of the real power of performance, and how it affected him physically and mentally.

"Over the years, I've read and researched the occult and magic. And I think the closest thing to that power that I've encountered is being onstage. It goes as far back as Julius Caesar: someone discovering the power that exists between a performer or leader and an audience. That's what I've experienced a lot and experimented with. And part of our show is a statement on that.

"It's very hard. I feel very drained after a performance, and not just physically. It takes a lot out of me mentally too. It's hard to deal with. Sometimes I have to be around people. Other times I can't be around anybody. It's different every day. It's never the same.

"I cannot be talked to or bothered for at least three hours before a show. I like to be myself and don't like to think about anything or anybody."

And in the *Kerrang!* interview with Paul Brannigan, he talked about his sexual feelings during a live performance.

"I feel very sexual onstage which is why I've got in trouble with my performance getting out of hand: the 'lewd and lascivious behaviour' as the authorities call it. When I get that energy from the audience, I can't control it sometimes. It's difficult to explain to someone who hasn't experienced it, but you kind of yield your control to another force."

Unsurprisingly, this jolted Brannigan's memory about the infamous fellatio incident involving Nine Inch Nails' guitarist. So what exactly were Manson's sexual persuasions? Or had he simply got carried away in the heat of the moment?

"I've never had a full-blown homosexual experience but a lot of things that have skated round the situation. More first base than going all the way, to use high school terminology. My experiences didn't happen in high school because I was unsure of myself altogether, never mind sexually. And I think high school is the worst time to experiment sexually because you haven't really developed your ideas of sexuality. My homosexual experiences have happened in recent years, now that I'm more confident about who I am."

As far as relationships were concerned, Manson told Brannigan that he didn't think it could be very easy going out with someone like him, although he was supposed to

"I CONSIDER MYSELF TO BE A DEATH SEX SYMBOL."

have had a girlfriend for the past five years. Marriage wasn't important to him, he said, and he didn't think love and sex had anything to do with each other, although he did admit to finding a 'significant other' very worthwhile.

And finally, did Marilyn Manson see himself as a sex symbol?

"I consider myself to be a death sex symbol."

Of course.

CHAPTER SIX

the reflecting god

*m*arilyn Manson's rise to fame has raised many questions about celebrity, entertainment, morals, religion, the power of rock culture and the hypocrisy which lies at the heart of many societies. His success has been phenomenal in a decade crying out for more and more extreme forms of entertainment, in an age where computer games and cinematic effects are reaching levels never before imagined. The spectacle created by Marilyn Manson has been enormous, and has had a profound influence on a generation looking for ways to upset their parents. Where Manson goes from here is anyone's guess, but if he has his way, he'll simply gain more strength, and continue with the success he's already built up.

Having put paid to the shy, repressed, maladjusted Brian Warner, Marilyn Manson has allowed his character to expand in ways he'd never have thought possible as an awkward, unpopular kid. And herein lies his real message – the one about following your dreams, and thinking for yourself. And if that means the devil ends up with even more of the best tunes, so be it.

THE REFLECTING GOD

marilyn manson